Saffire-Rose
Fletcher

Revive My Life
A Story For the Experienced

Volume 2

First published by Busybird Publishing 2022

Copyright © 2022 Saffire Rose-Fletcher

ISBN: 978-1-922691-92-7

This work is copyright. Apart from any use permitted under the *Copyright Act 1968*, no part of this publication may be reproduced, stored in a retrieval system or transmitted in any form or by any means, electronic, mechanical, photocopying, recording or otherwise, without the prior written permission of Saffire Rose-Fletcher.

Cover Image: Saffire-Rose Fletcher

Cover design: Busybird Publishing

Layout and typesetting: Busybird Publishing

Busybird Publishing
2/118 Para Road
Montmorency, Victoria
Australia 3094
www.busybird.com.au

I dedicate this book to
Jo Foster
and
Blaise van Hecke.

About the Author

Saffire-Rose Fletcher was born on the central coast of Australia in 1986.

She embarked on her journey as a singer/songwriter in 2013, turning her poems into songs, combining that with her (brief) piano knowledge, while also studying audio engineering and sound production.

Her lecturer identified that she had talent and that she was somebody to watch in the future.

As a means of further developing her craft, she used the open mic night scene as a training ground. It was a challenging period but also invaluable experience.

In 2015, Saffire moved to Melbourne (the musical capital of Australia) to pursue her dream of becoming an established and successful singer/songwriter.

Since then, Saffire has played over 250 gigs, recorded countless demos, directed and filmed her music videos, and has varied her musical genres by exploring the rock scene with her band 'SAFFIRE'.

It wasn't until late 2018, when Saffire discovered her true sound, which resembles EDM qualities.

Saffire's intention through her songs is to address topics that are overlooked in society – primarily in the realm of self-development, grief, forgiveness, self-love and, most of all, combatting adversity.

She has since become a qualified counselor, has embarked on some acting endeavours and has become a published author of two books: *Maybe I Can Rise Above* and *Revive My Life*.

Follow Saffire on Instagram, Twitter, YouTube, Tiktok and Facebook in order to find out more about her, her music, her two published books and where to purchase them.

Facebook:
www.facebook.com/saffireroseofficial/

Instagram:
www.instagram.com/saffirerosefletcher_official

Spotify:
open.spotify.com/artist/14xr80t6QNIrKCXxxdJmNA

Tiktok:
tiktok.com/@saffirerosefletcher

Twitter:
https://twitter.com/officialsaffire

YouTube:
www.YouTube.com/saffirerosefletcher

Contents

Introduction	1
Chapter 1 **Mission Abort**	7
Chapter 2 **Dark Night of the Soul**	19
Chapter 3 **Two Rib Surgeries During a Global Pandemic**	27
Chapter 4 **Time To Face the Music**	41
Chapter 5 **Rose-Coloured Glasses Removed**	51
Chapter 6 **A Test of Faith**	59
Chapter 7 **Give Me A Break!**	73
Chapter 8 **And Just Like That …**	87
Chapter 9 **Reviving My Life**	95
Acknowledgements	115
Resources	119

Introduction

This is a follow up of my previous book *Maybe I Can Rise Above*.

If you noticed, 'Maybe' is the operative word in that title. It's about me comfortably sitting in my failures and uncomfortable truths. It's a story about understanding damaged people, self-acceptance, overcoming adversity, and learning to love who you are, no matter what you've been through. Little did I know that I'd be continuing down a path that would challenge every one of my previous revelations.

As my journey progressed from *Maybe I Can Rise Above*, I found myself enduring a nervous breakdown, reliant on antipsychotics, antidepressants and pain relief following two painful and intense ribs surgeries.

And all this was during a global pandemic!

I almost died. With this harsh reality check, I had two options. The first option was obvious, surrender. My second option, was to stay.

I chose to stay.

I came off everything, all by myself. I also took life by the horns and transformed it.

I hope this story inspires people to speak up. To stand up. To rise up, and mostly, to not give up!

After you rise, you will indeed fall again. I learned this to be inevitable. In my case, I was on the peak of rising, only to fall the hardest I'd ever fallen … and it was brilliant!

Yes, that's right.

Brilliant.

Like first book, *Revive My Life* is not a self-help book. I find that many self-help books advise readers on the best way to accumulate financial status and power, yet this can be detrimental to an authentic healing process. We need to establish a mindset where we're grateful for the good that remains in our life. All that truly matters is what you're leaving behind, and that should only be kindness and compassion. The rest is a fleeting illusion.

Some of these self-help books proceed to inform you that you're lacking something so as to profit from your desire to heal. By teaching you that happiness can be purchased, or gained through becoming more than you are, these self-help books feed on your pain.

Surrender is a beautiful thing – trusting the process of your life, for example. But it must not be done with an intention to gain exteriorly.

I use the word 'exteriorly' as a reference to wanting to gain things via the means of outside gratification, rather than working on thyself from within in order to improve your life.

Surrender is purely designed to gain internally ... and that gain, my friend, is peace of mind and contentment!

Within this renewed concept, I discovered the true definition of rising above.

Might I also add that one person's story might not even be relevant or applicable to another person's individual journey. But I hope that you, the reader, are able to take something from my story.

Chapter 1

Mission Abort

Let's just say, 2020 was hardly scratching the surface of what was to come. The universe decided to turn the adversity up a notch.

A lot of good came out of 2020 and 2021 but it took some excruciating lessons in order for me to understand that I hadn't even grasped the true essence of self-healing. That is, until I experienced what's known as the dark night of the soul – a very abrupt and painful awakening process (as less spiritually inclined folk would describe the term).

'Dark night of the soul' is where you see or experience something that forever changes you. You cannot unsee something so dark in this world, and therefore it alters the way you see others, including yourself. Yet, it's the only way toward a positive transformation, unless you choose anger and seek revenge for enduring the torment – which isn't the solution!

The solution is to use the experience as a wakeup call and to proceed where there is light and authenticity. Detach yourself from physically pleasing exteriors, as they're no longer relevant once you've experienced such darkness. It was the most painful process of my entire life.

And trust me, I've lived a life!

I never felt more alone, more misunderstood, or more in danger of some very serious consequences regarding my health and my mental wellbeing than during the dark night of the soul.

It was slowly killing me.

Many years ago, I was told that I'm a light worker, which I'm happy to be, if so. Being a light worker requires shadow work, which relates to this particular phase that I endured. I'm about to share with you my own personal experience with the intention to debunk a lot of prejudices against this topic I'm passionate about. It's taken me a lot of internal work to release the shame that is created purely out of ignorance and fear – ignorance due to lack of experience, and fear of the unknown.

But there *is* plenty to fear. Not always the people, in reference to the topic that I'm about to speak upon, but the *experience*. I think by now you'd establish what I'm talking about, and that is the topic of addiction.

Speaking upon this topic, I feel compelled to state that people shouldn't feel ashamed for merely requiring some relief either physically, medically, intellectually, or emotionally! I mean, how ridiculous is that?

When you truly analyse it at its core, many people are doing imperfect things behind locked doors in their own way all around the world – they just don't disclose that information to everyone. It all comes down to miscommunication and misinformation. This is the problem!

But I ask, why is attempting to reduce pain of all forms something to be ashamed of? And most importantly, how is reducing someone to shame helping humanity? It only angers someone (who is already at their lowest) and causes them to be destructive towards either themselves or others.

I'm not here to make justifications to support the behaviour. I'm trying to break the deluded construct that addiction is filthy and you're a lost cause if you are, or have been *one of those people*, who depends on a particular substance in order to function throughout a challenging time. Shame is so easily spread throughout society like a virus ... no pun intended here!

In my humble opinion, escaping a mad world (in a pivotal point in history) shouldn't be a reason to carry any shame, especially regarding any choices you made during a global crisis. Things were very uncertain for many people: employment was strained, education was difficult, mental health took a hit, and seeking assistance during this time wasn't as organised and helpful as one would hope!

In all fairness, I don't think the medical industry anticipated the issues that needed rectifying within communities during the pandemic because they were so bombarded with patients, although, consequently, cases such as mine were highly misdirected. Hence, why I developed a dependence on prescription medication for undiagnosed pain that I will explain shortly.

Addiction, to me, means that you aren't currently strong enough to contend with what you're seeing and feeling in this crazy world, things that others cannot see nor comprehend. And this is what leads some people down very dangerous roads regarding their assumptions on this particular matter of addiction … especially when the advice that you're seeking isn't correct and your situation isn't assessed according to your individual circumstances. Instead, you're assessed via the means of outdated textbooks and theories, not proper facts.

Trust me, it's easy to say, 'It's a choice', as I've been guilty of stating in one of my songs! But when there are errors in the system, and the human condition is involved (regarding prescription medication), it's a fragile and delicate topic – one that needs identifying, addressing, and, most of all, compassion.

Not judgement.

If we've learned anything these days, it's that so many people are hiding pain and sorrow behind a facade while trying to retain the approval of others. This can be especially difficult for parents trying to maintain a certain lifestyle for their children and keep them fed.

Nobody truly knows what a person is feeling or thinking. But this is rarely taken into consideration. Also, the average person doesn't have time to dissect their internal battles and feelings outside of a counselling session. They're given one hour to unpack it all only to be further questioned, 'How does that make you feel?'

It's a question that still makes my blood boil to this very day. Most of the time, I'd be thinking upon being asked this question, *How the bloody hell would you feel?* Common sense is lacking without experience.

So this is a story for the experienced because it is only via the means of experience that you truly develop empathy! And empathy is required in order to comprehend somebody else's perspective. As I've always said, 'Everyone is coming from a different perspective.

You may notice that my opinions towards getting assistance have changed to an extent since my first book. I definitely believe there's proper help out there, but it can take some time to find somebody who is genuinely invested in your wellbeing and who will make it a pleasant experience for you, but only if they have the necessary experience – education is irrelevant if it's only based on textbooks. Life experience is the key!

But then again, I realised, that people were too busy fighting for themselves and their own families – they are all on their own journey and it isn't their responsibility to save me. I guess I just wished my family had reached out to me.

But this wasn't to be.

I like to believe that the universe was testing my resilience and I had no choice but to surrender to the adversities that I would further face. Sometimes, strength is your only choice. I mean, if, at 29 years of age, I could survive losing my mum (who was my only support system), handle all of her affairs by myself, be questioned by police, depart a toxic relationship in the midst of enduring some *savage* connections, move back and forth between two different states in a matter of weeks, and make a bold move to an entirely new state (with two bags to my name) all on my own, surely, I could conquer this.

Right?

This time, my fight was to be diagnosed, have surgery (in the middle of a global pandemic), and get off pain relief.

Yet every time I attempted to come off the tablets it was like everything that I was escaping heightened tenfold – the physical pain and my mental struggles were magnified, especially when responding to things I'd normally laugh at or agree with for the sake of keeping the peace. I began to recognise all the reasons why I enjoyed the escape.

During this time, I had many external challenges that were testing the strength of the progress I'd made in healing from my past. It was becoming very apparent that I still had much work to do and this took a toll on my self-esteem. I forgot everything I'd learned from my previous experiences, as everything was mirroring my past.

Needless to say, this only contributed to my desire to escape, so I increased the dosage of my medication on a daily basis because I just didn't want to *feel* anymore. But the fall wasn't worth the high. I like to think the only valuable thing that came from that experience was that it alleviated my physical pain for a while, and it helped me understand somebody else's perspective so I could share these revelations!

I felt so self-conscious of my weight loss, and every time somebody said I was 'too skinny' I started to understand the perspective of someone who cannot help their size. It's the opposite conundrum of someone who has extra weight on, although I imagine the feelings of embarrassment are very much the same.

Okay, so I need to go back into early 2020 to detail how certain events transpired. When the pandemic began, I started taking Valium after one phone consult that I organised with my GP. Gradually over a few weeks, I became addicted to not only pain relief, but of course, Valium as well.

Then, toward the end of 2020 my GP discharged me without warning. She didn't even inform me during our appointment, nor did the receptionists. She just cut me off!

Eventually, I found a new GP to consult regarding my issues and having them accommodated. I was prescribed a high quantity of Valium to take weekly, along with a box of Panadeine Forte. This prescription and my intake were never monitored or supervised. Again, in all fairness, there was much distraction around the pandemic. I don't think anyone could keep up with each patient's concerns and issues. So, I understand.

At the very end of 2020, this GP also abruptly cut me off without warning and provided me a letter of discharge stating that I was 'too complex' for her expertise, which is fair enough, but the abrupt halt regarding my addiction wasn't sensible! The side effects of that were horrendous: my weight was too low, my white blood cell count was down, and my body began to shut down. I felt like I was dying – I guess I was. I'll never forget the feeling. It's something that I wouldn't wish on anyone.

Too add more fuel to the fire, in early 2021 my psychiatrist discharged me. I was told that I was (yet again) 'too complex'. Lovely! I was only trying to fight for my life and process and accept my CPTSD during a pandemic. I also had to register that I was 'problematic' for seeking assistance regarding my panic attacks and night terrors, which related to echoes of my past trauma and the current climate.

I felt like I was an utter lost cause and abandoned by the system.

My withdrawal symptoms became so acute that I'd experience night sweats, bed sweats, bedwetting, irritation, formication, anxiety, and suicide ideation. I couldn't sleep or breathe alongside terrible chest pains and confronting thoughts … and all of this on top of my rib pain.

It wasn't until a couple of months later that I discovered this could have been prevented if my initial GP had structured a plan for me to withdraw from my medication gradually and appropriately.

In January 2021, Marilyn and I decided to give our relationship another shot. Marilyn was someone who I thought was my soulmate. We attempted to navigate cultural and religious implications that caused a turbulent halt to our relationship in 2020.

We lasted two months and proceeded to be friends and live together because of COVID-19. There was nowhere for me to go. I think we can all see that I was in no position to be in a relationship. I needed to work on myself, and Marilyn had her own work to do on herself as well.

Finally in February 2021 I was diagnosed with two fractured ribs and cartilage damage. I was booked in for rib surgery for late March of 2021 – all thanks to my decision to pull a ridiculous stunt like simultaneously singing and swinging from some bars whilst pulling my best P!nk impersonation.

Needless to say, acrobatics isn't my strong point. I am grateful, though, for being treated so efficiently during a pandemic whilst being on the public system! I was one of the lucky ones.

So, what happened as a consequence of not having an accurate analysis of my case during those 12 months? I became addicted to two substances prior to my surgery as a result of misdiagnosis and neglect.

I went to a new GP that was willing to wean me off Valium appropriately and eventually (post rib surgery) would wean me off pain relief too.

Of course, I defied his requests regarding the quantity that I would take weekly on several occasions. My body was accustomed to a particular dosage by this stage. It was extremely difficult to get into a proper rhythm of quitting Valium.

Especially due to an event that transpired in February 2021.

Chapter 2

Dark Night of the Soul

In late 2020, I ended up in hospital for chronic rib and chest pain numerous times that bled into 2021.

My mother died of a heart attack a few years prior so I have always been cautious about my heart health and any worrying symptoms. One time, I was admitted to hospital for drinking too much alcohol while on medication; I collapsed and hit my head.

The last reason I was admitted into hospital was because I was diagnosed with bronchitis a week before my rib diagnosis and a month before my surgery. I was so sick that I spent an entire week without any sleep due to coughing my lungs up.

I felt like I was dying, so I finally decided to get some assistance.

I'd met some lovely and patient nurses during those times I'd visited hospital. But, on my last occasion in particular, one nurse detested the ground I walked on. I'd never felt so hated in all my life and I had absolutely no idea as to why.

I appreciate that COVID-19 had left such a lasting impact on medical staff and coming back from that, only to incur some minor cases (such as mine) would be challenging … though no matter how much sympathy I had for this particular nurse, she continued to express her disdain for me in many ways.

The night I showed up with bronchitis was a night I'll never forget.

I overheard every negative word she said about me as I was placed in a COVID-19 secure emergency cubical (due to my symptoms) directly opposite reception. Not only was I confronted with the horrible words she had to say about me, but I also witnessed a dead body that was wrapped up being wheeled past my room. I'd never seen a dead body before.

My entire body went numb and heavy. I almost felt the weight of the vessel as it passed me. I was traumatised. I was two weeks off Valium and riddled with anxiety and panic! But the night was far from over…

I overheard the nurse request that every doctor that enters my room deny me of any tablets. She glowered at me from across reception like I was filthy and proceeded to suggest that I hadn't made any effort to see my psychologist, when in fact I'd committed to see her every single session. The question I had was, why was she even looking up such information regarding my mental health history? Especially when I was being held in emergency for a viral infection? It was entirely irrelevant! Then, she yelled 'Liar!' out from across reception.

I thought to myself, *She's directly accusing me of lying – what the heck?* I was treated with absolutely no humanity. My anxiety and coughing fits were cast aside as if I was crying wolf.

This is where past trauma needs to be considered and entered into your private file to prevent assumptions relating to each individual. We all have a story to tell and it only takes a couple of brief sentences to tell that story. I mean, my mother died of a heart attack so of course my concerns were merited and common among people with CPTSD.

This was the first time in a long time that I reverted to my younger experiences of feeling unsafe. I mean, who mocks mental health these days?

I was ostracised for taking a selfie (whilst laying down during my coughing fits – in between takes) in an attempt to connect to anyone who'd care on my social media accounts. This was considered a display of not being sick. *What?* Since when is reaching out for human connection when you're sick a crime? Or a sign of faking your illness?

This night was enough to tip me over the edge. I felt so alone with my thoughts and feelings – I'd finally cracked and I wanted out. So, when I came home early that morning, I decided I was about to take my own life.

I had pills sitting directly in front of me and I was so scared of what I might do with them. I didn't want to subject Marilyn to seeing this behaviour, so I compartmentalised and made sure Marilyn didn't witness the full extent of how I was feeling. I needed to suppress my emotions and stay composed. I called the ambulance for assistance, but they didn't take the matter seriously at first. I'm assuming it was because I was so calm, which is understandable in hindsight.

Finally, after much explanation about how I was feeling to the ambulance call centre, they finally agreed to collect me and take me into a psychiatric ward. When I entered the ambulance and they transported me to the ward, I felt like I was being interrogated and everyone was against me – except for Terrence, one of the ambulance drivers, who I'll never forget.

Inside the psychiatric ward, it was very clean, the smell was very clinical, and everything appeared just like you'd see in the movies. I had a protection belt placed upon my stretcher in case I became of any harm to myself or others. Then, I was placed for an hour next to a lady who suffered schizophrenia.

Terrence offered to grab me a cup of water, twice. He proceeded to ask me questions about a book that I mentioned I was having published mid-2021. He was an angel and kept reassuring me that everything would be okay.

Once they established that I wasn't of any harm to anyone, and I had calmed down a little, they discharged me. I was prescribed a script for six Valium. After two weeks without it, I was once again craving and back on the wagon of reducing my intake. Not only that, but I lost 3 kilos in one night due to the stress and was paranoid and high-strung for weeks. Nothing could calm me down. Not even Valium.

A few days later, a new psychiatrist prescribed me a high dose of anti-psychotics and a new form of therapy was set into place for me two weeks later.

It was apparent that I'd had a breakdown – thanks to extended medication use, withdrawals, COVID-19, my CPTSD diagnosis, another break up, my surgeries during lockdown, dark night of the soul, and revising my first book during lockdown to finally have it published. It was a lot.

Speaking to my former psychologist in the interim of connecting with new assistance was painful because she couldn't save me, nor help me on the matters that were truly frightening me. I had never felt more alone, and I was terrified of what was to become of me.

Of course, I had no friends to reach out to, so I reached out to my family for the first time in a quite a while. I sent a desperate cry for help via a recorded video of myself crying on Facebook. It entailed my wishes for everyone to believe that they are enough, so that they'd have a reminder that I held no ill will toward them in case anything ever happened to me. Safe to say, I was at my lowest.

Nobody replied.

Nevertheless, my surgery was approaching, I was a Category A, 47 kilos in weight, frail, pale and very weak.

I was declining rapidly.

I had no choice but to be strong on my own!

Chapter 3

Two Rib Surgeries During a Global Pandemic

During my initial consultations with my new psychiatrist, psychologist, and social worker, I was classified at crisis point, a place I'd never been before.

I walked into the doctor's clinic where my new GP practiced for one of my weekly appointments. Experiencing intense hand and body tremors, I approached the receptionist and informed her that I didn't feel stable on my feet.

Just days earlier, my blood test results came back stating that I had an overactive thyroid and low blood sugar – another physical symptom I'd never endured before. This was primarily due to the stress my body was under. Whenever I walked, I felt as if I'd faint. And, believe me, I was shovelling fatty and nutritional food down to keep my body functioning to maximum capacity. You know you're in trouble when your doctor says to you, 'Saffire, please stay alive.'

Upon waiting for the day of surgery to arrive, I was incredibly anxious and fragile. The pain was worsening by the minute and I felt very weak. The pandemic was causing a lot of setbacks, even though I was a Category 1 patient. Although I'm grateful I was seen at all given it was through public health.

This receptionist had the kindest nature as she took me to lay down in a discreet little surgical room. Her hands touched my own with much care and compassion. I felt safe and understood for at least a moment.

Once my doctor saw me, he agreed to commence a well-structured plan to decrease my painkiller and Valium intake, but I wasn't to be taken off any of these tablets until I had my rib fixation surgery.

Finally, the day of my surgery arrived, and I never felt more terrified of being in hospital completely alone during a pandemic. It was mayhem; the nurses were overworked and exhausted from their attempt to keep up with the demands of patients. Of course, this chaos only intensified my tremors and anxiety.

Aggravated patients yelled and swore at the hospital staff for the most mundane circumstances. Granted, I think a lot of people in the hospital were also suffering mental health obstacles like myself. They just externalised their feelings more abrasively.

The one thing I was looking forward to was being put under sedation because then my anxiety would be non-existent.

Right before I was sedated I made a few jokes with the surgeons and fellow staff to lighten the stress. They appreciated a much easier and pleasant patient. But I was terrified that I may not wake up due to my current weight and declining health.

When I did wake up, I was in agony. I was crying loudly as I'd never experienced such pain, so they increased my pain relief. Whilst I waited in recovery, I tried to fight the fatigue because I felt unsafe with my surroundings. Outside of my room, people continued to yell for the doctors and nurses. But despite my own pain, I felt sorry for everyone involved.

I hadn't been able to pass urine for the entire day, so the nurses attempted to place a catheter into my bladder whilst I was completely awake. Being a virgin and all, I was immensely triggered and could feel the onset of a panic attack. The catheter was so painful that they couldn't complete the job. So, I asked for a toilet chair to get the job done myself. It took many minutes but I finally had relief. Yet, I was still shaken up by the experience not to mention getting up for the first time was incredibly painful.

I was finally taken to my room where a few other people rested post-surgery I was placed near the window. I couldn't sleep on my side or back as the pain was unlike anything I could describe. I couldn't find a comfortable position without the risk of ripping the dissolvable stitches. I now had internal metal ribs with mesh coverings to protect the hardware.

The following day a new patient was placed beside me. Her name was Jo. We quickly bonded; she reminded me very much of my mother. Whenever I'd leave my bed to go to the bathroom, she would spray my bed with a nice calming essence and surprise me with my favourite treats, a small statue of an angel and a freshly brewed coffee. Everyday! She was a godsend, and I felt like I had a guardian angel beside me. We also had regular nurses who were also angels to everyone.

I decided to make an awfully slow and painful walk downstairs to the newsagency to buy Jo and my fellow patients some presents and cards to lighten their spirits. Everyone had each other's back, and it was honestly a lovely and humbling experience despite the pain we were all in.

Whilst many of my nurses, like the ones I mentioned earlier, were angels, I did find that I had some negative experiences. I encountered a few nurses who weren't as pleasant and who interrogated my Valium usage. I was very switched on and told them who my psychiatrist was and that I was also being treated for CPTSD.

I stated this with no shame. One nurse's attitude changed quickly when I stated the facts with confidence and clarity.

Then, another nurse appeared on my fifth day declaring that it was time to go home. Her reasoning was that I was well enough to make the effort and the journey to get everyone tea and coffee, so I was clearly well enough to go home. I informed her I was merely trying to reduce the strain and pressure on the staff and that my kind heart shouldn't indicate that I was in any lesser pain as a result.

Another time, I had Marilyn's father visit me to accuse me of lying about my health. I quickly lifted up my dressing gown and showed him my horrendous scar, saying, 'If this a lie, then why would I be a Category A if I were faking it?'.

I assumed it was the make-up I was wearing in order to look half alive, so I told him make-up hides a lot of things. I applied make-up with my hand-held mirror to hide how pale and sick I was. I was so scared to be unappealing. I was already in a fragile position and my self-esteem wasn't exactly 100%. Strange, hey? You wear make-up and people automatically think you look well, even when you weigh 47 kilos, are pale, frail and just days post-surgery.

These experiences were not pleasant. But I was grateful upon my discharge from hospital for the good people that I shared my experience with. I was in there for five days due to the severity of my pain. Jo was in there for longer, as she just had open heart surgery.

During this time, lockdown was a little less intense and Marilyn was able to visit once a day for an hour. I appreciated that, although she would get upset if I called her when I was lonely or triggered by the hospital events that were transpiring. I eventually learned that calling her or messaging her was off limits. She would complain that there was always something wrong, always a reason to call, and she seemed to be sick of it.

I couldn't understand what I was doing so wrong. I just needed a friend, someone who cared. It was lockdown and being in a hospital environment post-surgery was difficult – especially when you have no family or friends reaching out to you to see if you're okay. Not to mention, I had an online friend who turned on me post-surgery, stating that she felt pressured to be there for me whilst I was recovering. I decided to not even acknowledge it, because I didn't even know where that came from and why someone would even say such a thing when someone is in recovery from a big surgery. I had never asked anyone to be there for me, especially someone I had never met.

Thankfully, Jo was there, and I knew I was finally aligning with like-minded, beautiful souls who had no intention of hurting or wounding me. Jo and I proceeded to keep in contact and catch up to this very day.

When I returned home, I received some interesting messages from people telling me what to do – not relating to my health, though. It was more relating to my personal life and choices. Nobody reached out to see how my recovery was going.

It was an interesting time, so I decided to make some new friends through an online dating site. I had many funny discussions under the influence of pain-killers, and let's just say it wasn't boring. I encountered some very savage people and re-learned some old lessons about trusting people way too soon. But during this time, it was nice to just not feel, in which case I understood the need for escapism (as I originally addressed in my first chapter).

In March of 2021, my book *Maybe I Can Rise Above* was released on Amazon and other book-related platforms. I had never felt more encouraged to put my legacy out into the world and to help others feel less alone with their thoughts and experiences. I generated 46 sales (worldwide) in three months and received some wonderful feedback. Not bad for a start.

Three months later, my pain was worse than before my surgery and I couldn't gain any weight because the metal plates and screws were too tight around my rib cage. My surgeon admitted me back into hospital where I stayed for observation and awaited nerve injections for an entire week.

I was placed in a ward with people with intense psychological issues. I didn't sleep the entire time I was there. People were yelling, frustrated by the lengthy delays in between nurses, but this only caused further distress as the nurses were under so much pressure and demand. But there was also panic as no one was allowed any visitors. My anxiety was heightened, and I was struggling both emotionally and physically.

Seven days later, I had three nerve injections in my ribs and I was discharged, only to incur no improvement. Despite this, I gave my surgeon a crystal tree from the crystal shop and one of my published hardcopies to her as a thank you, but she couldn't do anything for me from that point onwards. My issue was above her expertise. I'm still very grateful for her efforts regardless.

I tried to cope and get by without any assistance for about a week, but every time I attempted to fill my stomach with food to gain weight and increase my strength, my stomach would expand and cause crippling pain.

Eventually, I was able to find a new surgeon. He turned out to be the teacher of my former surgeon and said that rib fixation surgery is an outdated method of approach and that he doesn't recommend it. Granted, it was too late now, so the only option was to remove the hardware.

He could see how much pain I was in and was concerned about my current weight. I'd never been so frail in all my life. My new surgeon booked me in for another Category A surgery almost immediately. Two weeks later, I was in a new hospital awaiting my second surgery of 2021.

To make matters worse, just a few days before surgery my cat unexpectedly started vomiting blood. She was my rock during that year. Marilyn and I quickly rushed Cookie to the vet, only to hear that she had passed away of a heart attack.

I'll never forget seeing her so distressed and looking at me as if she was saying, *Help me, Mum*. I got to hold her in my arms one last time and I kissed her on the forehead and said goodbye. I just couldn't believe this was happening.

Later, before my surgery, I shed a few tears in the waiting room prior to entering the operating theatre. I was thinking about Mum, wishing she was here with me, and grieving the loss of Cookie.

What a year, hey?

When I woke up from my second surgery of 2021, I was in pain, but I could feel less tension around my ribcage, which was positive news. I was placed in recovery next to a lady who was unravelling significantly. She was swearing at the staff and calling them terrible names.

One of the nurses saw how triggered and terrified I was because the lady beside me was about to become very violent. Security was called and the nurse held my hand to reassure me that I was safe. I told her I suffer from CPTSD and my experiences in hospital during lockdown hadn't been the most pleasant in terms of fellow patients.

No visitors were allowed still, and I had to wait five hours before I could reclaim my phone and wallet to pay for TV usage. Until then, I had nothing to do but stare at the ceiling. Everyone appeared to be experiencing the same distress. My anxiety was so heightened that I thought the nurses had lost my phone (the only source of connection to the outside world). But I was finally reunited with my belongings later in the night.

A few of the new friends I had made through a lesbian dating site suffered mental health battles themselves, and I was kept up some nights in hospital by a few issues that were arising in their lives. I completely empathise with their fears and anxieties as I too have been there. But being in hospital in immense pain and anxieties myself, I found it challenging, although I continued to do my best to provide them a source of comfort.

I was gifted many things by these new friends whilst being in there. Whilst I never asked for anything, I was grateful nonetheless, although after a while, odd things started to occur.

One of my new friends, Stacey, decided to block my other friend, Andy, on social media and this caused a rift between me and Andy, who I had helped move here just weeks prior to my surgery. I handled most of her affairs and made sure her house had all her furniture delivered. I even lent her money and took her for many drives all around the city to show her around, so she felt less alone during her first weeks without a car. And I did all this despite being in incredible pain.

We had promised to always remain friends no matter what, but she turned on me without warning in the midst of my recovery just because somebody that I was briefly talking to blocked her online.

She thought I'd said or done something behind her back. I hadn't; I was flabbergasted. Already distracted by the grief of losing my cat and enduring lockdown in hospital after my second surgery of the year, I wouldn't have had the energy. Plus, it's not my style to speak negatively behind someone's back. So, to say that I was heartbroken and disappointed is an understatement.

I had absolutely no idea what was going on. There was a lot of drama and no genuine time for me to rest. When I reflected on the gifts I received in hospital, I felt as if I was being claimed and like it was some kind of competition regarding who provided me the best gifts. Everything was just so premeditated and strange.

Those friendships didn't last because of too much high school drama, harsh words expressed to me (unexpectedly post-surgery) and lack of constructive communication. In retrospect, I do consider that they were dealing with their own demons and something which I represented was triggering to them. They are still decent people.

But it was becoming very apparent that I had to do this on my own and it was bloody tough to say the least! I felt very alone and fragile. Yet, I had to carry on with my own healing journey.

Chapter 4

Time To Face the Music

During my healing process and lockdown with Marilyn, I came to some conclusions about myself and how I've navigated life.

Every romantic relationship and friendship I've had, I would always immediately trust and surrender my cards all without any effort or proof supporting the other person's promises to me. I would plummet into an unhealthy pattern of false security that provided me a momentary high, only to fall twice as hard.

Marilyn was wonderful in some respects (which I'll clarify more on later in this book), but the romance and love we once had for each other wasn't there anymore ... and that's okay. We fought a lot during lockdown, and I discovered many differences between us, differences I just couldn't live with anymore. I could no longer live the lie. For the first time in my life I just wanted to be free;. I craved for my own haven where I could just be myself and feel safe.

The concept of love and friendship was changing for me as I'd been burned a lot by many people during this stage, especially regarding my mental health. I was coming to terms with the potential fact that I might be destined to do life completely alone, like Mum did.

I concluded that nobody would ever truly understand me nor would ever be able to provide me with the love that I can provide for myself, and that I needed to be okay with that.

But this revelation didn't last long, though. Vulnerability rears its ugly head and attracts some vultures when you're at your lowest.

Nevertheless, for the first time in a long time, I had butterflies in my stomach and I felt alive again – for a moment anyway! Although Melbourne once again went back down into lockdown due to coronavirus, I had been accepted to study a Bachelor of Music!

During my rib surgery recovery, it was time to withdraw from painkillers permanently, because my ribs were finally fixed – well, they were still incredibly painful, but fixed. I also had to withdraw from the anti-psychotics I was on – what a shitstorm! I felt like I was dying.

I couldn't sleep; I had seizures, restless legs, night sweats, sleep paralysis, nausea, diarrhea, hot and cold flushes, and I felt like I had bugs crawling underneath my skin. I was riddled with anxiety and experienced copious panic attacks and cramps, and I was only two weeks away from beginning my studies. I had to even force myself to eat.

I wanted to die and even considered killing myself. It was that bad! But I kept a lot of it from Marilyn – until one day I experienced a full panic episode in front of her.

My hands seized up into crab claws and I hyperventilated. I cried to Marilyn as I sat on the bathroom floor, 'I can't do this; I don't want to be here anymore – it's too much. I cannot take anymore adversity.'

Marilyn had just started working full time at a job she was loving, and I was at home by myself a lot – something which I wanted prior, but with it being during lockdown while coping with my withdrawals, it was bloody *hard*. I wanted the complete opposite, even if there were disagreements, I didn't want to be alone. (Again, I commend people with former experiences with dependencies for overcoming it.)

Nevertheless, Marilyn suggested taking a few days off and, all of a sudden, I realised that this was impacting her. I wasn't going to be responsible for that.

I said, 'No, if you stay here, I'll never fully recover.'

I knew I had to do this on my own and not get in the way of her future. I had to step up and take control of my emotions because somebody else's life would be compromised as a result of mine. It wasn't her responsibility to provide me comfort or save me.

I was determined to fight the little shits.

I resorted to listening to positive affirmations on YouTube and was selective with the music I listened also. I listened to music from people who'd overcome adversity similar to my own in order to relate. Everything had to have a positive undertone because my outside influences were reflecting a different narrative. Music was the one thing that restored my resilience.

I also watched YouTube videos of people who had come off prescribed medication and how they triumphed over it. It inspired me.

I declared that whatever came my way in the future, I never wanted painkillers ever again – no way in hell! The withdrawals and the potential of my declining health wasn't worth it. Plus, as I mentioned, I didn't want to impact Marilyn negatively. I was still residing in her house after all.

So, I was off everything by this stage. Except for the occasional Valium if I felt like I was about to have a panic attack. I had improved.

Regardless of my efforts, Marilyn and I fought more than usual. I guess lockdown was taking its toll on our friendship, and if I'm honest, I missed the love and affection we once had for one another – even with the conflicting desire to be alone and independent arose.

I acknowledge I was a bit of a nag and a pain in the ass toward the end of our time living together. My drinking on weekends, subjecting her to long chats whilst she was trying to sleep, watching music videos on YouTube, and vomiting only for her to clean it up. I own that. I just wish she'd own her shortcomings and what lead to that.

I'm not making excuses, but just trying to kindly suggest that there are two stories here. In fact, there are many stories that a lot of readers would entirely understand and find flabbergasting to a huge degree. But I'm not repeating the same narrative I've always depicted in previous relationships. All we need to know is, yes, it happened again. Different person. Same situation.

I can simply say this: the fairy-tale I once told you that she provided me was anything but that. I was merely trying to protect her and her family, and I didn't want to throw anyone under the bus.

I was trying to convince myself if what a psychic told me about finding my soulmate was true, and was indeed Marilyn, because she resembled the images that were stated in the psychic's reading. So, to feel like I was on track in all areas of my life, I held onto the belief system that Marilyn was *my* soulmate, when really, she was just mirroring all the healing I had yet to accomplish.

Marilyn and I also had a lot of cultural and financial pressures to contend with. Everything was against us. It didn't bring out the best in us behind closed doors and it depleted any sense of self-worth I had left.

If I could go back in time, I'd never have entered that relationship. We both weren't ready, and my desperate need to be loved blinded my vision on what I had truly entered.

I had not healed from my past and it was reflected into this new relationship. There was no giving way. Although she did want to try again, she just didn't have it in her.

I longed to be held, kissed, and loved again so deeply. I felt even more worthless by this point.

Everything her family and friends thought of me would prove to be an accurate representation of me, but I had goals, I actioned those goals, and I was kind even whilst under the influence of alcohol and painkillers. (Inconsiderate of her sleeping pattern, yes ... but still loving and gentle.)

In my defence, considering the circumstances that I was subjected too, I had merit. I couldn't handle the pressure I was under regarding circulating issues that were raised during our relationship and post break-up. It was too much on top of my mental health and physical health obstacles. Plus, a pandemic! I mean, let's get real here!

In hindsight, I now see I wasn't perfect, but I know in my heart I was a good partner and friend. So, I'm less hard on myself now for my shortcomings. Regardless, it was doomed to fail, despite all both our efforts to still live together.

But change was coming.

I started rehearsing again (despite the pain I was in). I kept pushing on and I even wrote a new song relating to the recent adversity I'd conquered titled 'I Am Thor'. I would sing my songs again and would feel elation after I finished my new song. I was *happy*!

I knew from this point onwards I had made the right decision to return to music and give it one last shot. If I failed, at least I'd have a bachelor's degree and I'd be able to teach one day. I wasn't afraid of how crazy people thought I was anymore. I'd rather be a happy person dreaming of impossible things than an unhappy person doing what was hurting my soul. With the events that occurred during 2020 and 2021, I think many people came to that same conclusion.

I'd finally reached a level of understanding about what was truly happening around me and I started to ask myself the big questions, such as, *What about me?*, *What's in this for me? Why can't I achieve my dreams?* and *Why don't I deserve better?*

Those questions are the correct questions to ask yourself when you've spent a lifetime constantly moulding yourself to fit in with the people and surroundings around you in order to appease them based on your conditioning.

So, it turned out that my life would transform (instantaneously) once I decided that the only person who could save me was indeed ... *me!*

I started to see the value in what I'd been through, and it taught me how much I'm capable of. I realised how short life was and that no more time was to be wasted on robbing myself of a good life – especially after everything I had endured, both in and out of hospital.

It was time to thrive, not only survive!

Chapter 5

Rose-Coloured Glasses Removed

Once I finally stood back and chose *me* (even in the realm of friendship with an ex), my reality finally become apparent. Suddenly, I was more aware of my environment and the reality I had become accustomed to because of fear. I feared what would happen to me if Marilyn weren't to exist in my life anymore.

If I'm honest, I feared being alone and destitute if I allowed myself to see things for what they were.

I need to make this point before I complete my explanation on this matter: *Never mistake the universe and its intentions for you.*

It's holding you back for a reason. Don't fight it. Trust it. Embrace the lessons and let the universe catch up with your teachings. Once you've understood the lesson and what it has taught you, the universe will propel you forward into your next chapter. This is something I've observed throughout the duration of my life.

Nevertheless, my rose-coloured glasses were removed.

There is a lot of things that went down within the dynamics of our relationship, things that I promised her I'd never disclose, things that nobody else knew about her. So out of principle, despite how much she's hurt me. I won't reveal. Though I will add minor context as to why I made the decision to leave.

I think I'd reached my limit when the topic of my mother was raised at Marilyn's family dinner table on the eve of my mother's birthday. We were meant to be celebrating her life, and yet Marilyn's folks were commenting on her weight and how she wasn't very pretty. No, they didn't ask her what her favourite flower was. They were asking why she was fat and Marilyn never defended neither her nor me. I could cop insulting comments from her folks and Marilyn, but to mention my mother in that manner, that's when it hit me – these weren't my people. I had to leave.

One thing Marilyn once told me was that I'd never survive without her. Well, something inside me knew that I could.

I left her house.

There was a timely catalyst to my escape. Tara, a new friend that I had made online, had a family member with an unoccupied spare room just an hour away from my current location. So I packed up everything that belonged to me and left. It was painful. It took me an hour to leave the driveway.

Marilyn said everything was on me, and even though I sent her beautiful messages indicating I'd still be in her life, owning my shortcomings and stating that I'd be there for her if she ever needed me, she disregarded them and asked for me to return her keys.

I even reached out to her family, but they never responded. To all of them I was the villain. The drop-kick. Good riddance. No self-reflection. Just pity for Marilyn.

I was angry, disappointed, and hurt. But I internalised it. I spent my time fixated on my work and I developed feelings for my new friend. We explored it. I felt wanted, sexy and free.

Old habits die hard, right?

I was recording at Pony Studios in Melbourne with an amazing producer on my first debut EP, I had a solid band, and we'd practice in the same rehearsal studio Ed Sheeran did when he once toured Melbourne.

Everything felt perfect.

I was living in a beautiful apartment with my friend's relative and it had a magical view of the city skyline. Everything was just perfect (minus the incoming bills and incurring debt).

Leaving Marilyn and the cats was incredibly difficult. But when the day arrived, I was ready because I'd been subconsciously grieving that loss even years prior. I just couldn't leave due to COVID-19 restrictions, and the timing wasn't right. Plus, there was no chance of reconciling our differences.

When we did get back together in early 2021, for two months, she wouldn't even try to be affectionate or intimate with me. Whenever I'd try to communicate my feelings on the matter she'd aggressively dismiss me or laugh it off, depending on her attitude for that day.

I felt so unwanted.

I guess this contributed to my desire for Tara. I got lost in one connection, whilst escaping another. Tara told me everything I longed to hear.

But I only ever really wanted to hear it from Marilyn.

The week of my move was highly stressful. I got a car fine for parking in the wrong parking lane on the curb whilst selling my previous engagement ring for $350 at Cash Converters. I also had to manage all my commitments and organise my band rehearsals, complete a strenuous photoshoot with a photographer and record two singles, as well as commit to studies.

To add fuel to the fire, my phone also decided to die during my busiest week of the year and I had to update all my details with every resource I was utilising due to the recent move.

Then Marilyn asked me to pay her additional money knowing very well I was on a disability pension at the time for my CPTSD and rib surgeries. I'd already given her $12,000 over the course of our separation whilst living with her.

The thing that upset me the most is I never took anything that wasn't mine nor asked her for any money – like her most recent exes did and she gave them the money. She knew very well that I was now on my own yet targeted me because she knew I'd buckle.

After all this time, even our friendship meant nothing to her. She favoured money so much that she sabotaged any hope of a future friendship. I lost respect for her in her quest.

Regardless, I created a payment plan to commit to whatever she believed I owed her. I just wanted it over with and guilt of her carrying me during part of our relationship took a hold. I'd helped her out significantly with her business and was low maintenance regarding electricity and daily showering and food intake. Plus, there was no rent to pay because her father bought her a house. There's a fine line here. Still, I decided to do the right thing.

In honour of what we had, and despite my anger during this time in relation to Marilyn's behaviour toward me, there were some good aspects to Marilyn's personality despite all the turbulence. Her vulnerable side was the most precious, in my opinion, and I'm sure I wasn't easy to understand at times myself. But I saw a therapist, got help, did everything I could to salvage what we had, and it still made no difference.

I refrain from holding any guilt or shame here. I really tried my best. I never once asked her to seek treatment for her emotional obstacles. It was all on me to improve, which wasn't entirely fair. But, hey, it's done, and I learned a lot about my limitations in a relationship going forward, such as, how to be mindful when people purchase or do things for you, and how it can be used against you when things turn sour.

I'll end this chapter by saying that I'm immensely grateful for everything Marilyn taught me, and I wish her nothing but the best, I truly do. I learned a lot from her and again, she did have great qualities. But we just weren't compatible. We had different values, belief systems and, again, culture and religion can play a huge role in the divide regarding love.

Marilyn was enough.

I was enough.

We just weren't right for each other and that is more than okay.

Chapter 6

A Test of Faith

My new friend Tara bought me a couple of return flight tickets to Tasmania for December 2021 and January 2022. I accepted as I really needed a break away from all that had transpired, and I thoroughly enjoyed her company during our Facetime chats.

We had a connection that I'd never experienced before. It truly threw my world upside down. It wasn't love but something else. She awoke something within me, something sexual and spiritual. I thought it was love at the time. I felt safe to express my sexuality and I felt like a woman – nothing crazy; I felt sexy and free.

Mind you, we hadn't even met yet as she lived interstate. It's a crazy story and I took a leap of faith living with Tara's relative prior to meeting her, that's for sure. But I was desperate to escape my situation.

As you can see, I'm about to contradict my latest epiphany here. But I've always been very candid about my development. This was a momentary relapse in judgement on my part, and with all that had previously transpired, it was bound to happen. Who knows? Perhaps I was having another nervous breakdown?

Again, old habits die hard, right?

Tara and I got so caught up in our connection that we planned to get married the following year in January 2022. I met her parents and everything – it was a hot mess!

Yes, we'd only known each other for several weeks. All I'll say is that after all this time of wanting to be a wife and for someone to upgrade my title, it was confirmed that I no longer wanted to settle down anymore. Well, not until I got my shit together and truly stood on my feet, entirely independent and stabilised – and for the *right reasons*.

With much turbulence relating to our connection, and upon finally meeting in person post-lockdown, it was apparent that it was a bad choice to proceed with the engagement. She informed me well before our connection ignited that she had some communicational barriers. Yet I genuinely thought I had the skillset to manage it and work with it.

I was sincerely misguided.

It triggered so many suppressed emotions within me that the old version of myself was revealed in minor increments in terms of my defence mechanisms. I couldn't comprehend half of the things that came out of her mouth, and she had many moments of flaring up in front of my eyes, triggering my CPTSD. It was aggressive and I was starting to see red flags. She was a good person for the most part, but she had much healing to do.

Things weren't pretty in terms of events representing my past. I guess the universe was testing me to see if I'd really learned anything. A valuable re-enactment indeed.

The major red flags for me were when she asked if I'd disconnect from my friend Jo. Tara said that she always wanted someone who had no family so that that person would make her their primary focus. Meaning: *she wanted someone like myself, someone without family or a huge support system.* Sacrificing my friendship for Jo was something I'd never even contemplate, so I responded, 'No'.

We proceeded for a brief time. Then, little things, like me attempting to take care of her whenever she was sick by simply getting her a juice, would be met with hostility and a scowl. I tearfully walked away in in utter confusion. The person I had known on the internet was unlike anything she depicted in reality.

She was unhappy with what I wore, my hair, the list could go on. Then whenever we'd disagree, or whenever I'd call her out on it, she'd attempt reverse psychology (very poorly I might add) and then try to overcompensate by buying me gifts whenever she realised I wasn't caving in. She told me that if I rejected her gifts, I'm rejecting her love.

I mean, really?

Within three years I had two people with money attempting to buy my love.

But I never wanted that.

I just wanted *love*.

Despite all these negativities we attempted to remain friends and proceeded to get to know one another platonically – a very sensible decision if you ask me.

I know, right, what were we thinking?

(P.S. her folks were lovely to me at first. But then they started becoming controlling and forcefully projected their desires for me to be her wife one day. They didn't want Tara to end up a lonely old lady without anyone to care for her.)

I mean, really? I finally had parents' approval – but as a caretaker?

Many guilt trips and statements were made to make me feel bad. But I recognised the behaviour and didn't back down, though I remained kind and diplomatic despite the awkwardness.

Little did I know I'd be ending my year in an entirely new state of Australia.

Everything about this year had become exhausting as there was so much to process. I was physically, emotionally, and mentally drained.

I had nothing left.

Many dramas occurred, but I won't go into all that because if I've learned anything now it's that energy is precious. So, I'll preserve it here.

The conclusion to the story is that this brief connection fizzled quickly. I learned a lot about myself, and I was becoming more assertive and more aware of what I wanted in life, although it was tested every day and never remained consistent.

One thing I learned throughout this experience was that I no longer wanted to be answering to anyone, and for the first time in my life I was craving my *freedom*.

I missed my solitude! And someone touching me, making me feel wanted and sexy was not worth all this drama. Of course, it was lonely sometimes, but it was better than walking around warily and adjusting myself to fit someone else's life. I just needed to breathe. What a precious gift to receive after such a tiring soul-searching journey. Yes, maybe one day true love might be on the cards for me. But it was no longer something I was hoping or yearning for. Perhaps I was a little jaded at this point.

I kept looking back at 'old Saff' and thinking of all the years I'd wasted searching for love when my attention could have been elsewhere, focusing on progression, although I couldn't maintain that regret as it would deter me. Everything happens for a reason, and I wouldn't be as enlightened as I feel that I am today without these experiences.

Experience is key to growth, after all. And plus, without these lessons I wouldn't have all this *riveting content* to provide you all.

Perhaps this final development was only to provide me with confirmation of my previous revelations. Nevertheless, it was all in favour of my growth and I absorbed every lesson with gratitude.

The start of 2022 was a little edgy. Band members were coming and going, and COVID-19 cases were increasing by the minute; things were a little tense between my new housemate and I, plus I was losing gigs and losing bandmates.

I packed the boot of my car with toiletries and a suitcase full of clothes just in case I was unexpectedly asked to move out. I didn't know what to expect from this point onwards. I was constantly on edge.

Finding new band members proved to be difficult as most people in the music community were losing motivation (understandably). One of my band members had injured his wrist and so he had to withdraw from the band. Yet I still maintained a professional relationship with him as he was also producing my new EP.

But I was lucky enough to maintain one awesome member who played guitar for me, and we had backing tracks to replace the instruments that were missing in our live set. Nevertheless, our gigs were postponed as venues were justifiably hesitant to open their doors during (what was now becoming) precedented times.

Anyway, I decided to go on a quest to find more fellow bandmates (primarily a pianist) just in case the backing tracks lost their appeal to a live audience. Most of my interviews with potential bandmates crossed many of my boundaries and triggered some old wounds from my past trauma.

Specifically, I found many men who responded to my advertisements were merely wanting to meet me for underlying reasons. They'd suggest things that were leaning towards romantic or sexual intentions. Some of the suggestions and statements really made me uncomfortable.

One man even stalked me after a meeting and proceeded to call me countless times trying to build a more personal bond with me.

I was less tolerant and became less lenient with how I interacted with applicants because it was crossing a line and draining the energy that I wanted to use for music, and music alone.

It's harder to maintain a professional rapport when gender is involved. I guess that could apply to any number of industries regarding women. I started to wonder if I'd ever catch a break in the realm of gathering a proper and established band together due to the unfortunate fact of being a woman in the music industry.

I found myself reduced back to my younger self and the emotions that were attached to my comfort zone. Though now I was identifying them, and I was more aware and assertive of what I was seeing and what I would never tolerate again. I set my intentions and set my boundaries instantaneously before any future dramas could occur, as I'd been there many times before.

The silver lining to all of this was that I was finally coming into my own and I was starting to accept my own ability to survive without another person defining my existence or providing me with a false sense of security, be it was a bandmate, friendship, or relationship.

Unfortunately, more adversities were to come. My beautiful friend Jo contracted COVID-19. The idea of losing her devastated me, as it would feel like losing another mother.

When she called me, I attempted to hold back my tears but I broke down. I apologised as I didn't want her to feel like she had troubled me, and I wanted her to know I'd be mentally and emotionally there for her no matter what. The last thing she needed was to worry about my wellbeing, which is something she would do as she is simply that type of person – always thinking about and putting others before herself.

So, I regrouped and stepped away from my own feelings of distress and concern for her. I too had come in to contact with a positive COVID-19 case not long afterwards, but thankfully I tested negative, although, I was awfully sick and bedridden for two days straight.

At the time, I was also hit with the pressure of my debts. I wanted to pull myself together and make lemonade out of lemons. I chose to adjust to every adversity with an attitude of gratitude so the lessons would propel me forward in a constructive manner, despite how alone I felt at times on the journey.

I made a repayment plan for everyone I owed money to. Of course, repayments would be very little, but I set the intention and created a fortnightly schedule for payments to be deducted from my bank account – at least until I earned more money, as I was still hustling my way toward my dreams.

To add to my concerns, my ribs were flaring up again as a result of all the rehearsing I was doing, and I was resorting to prescribed CDB oil to manage my pain. But it didn't work, and it was very costly. I ended up on minor painkillers again for a very short period of time, until I started to realise how it was affecting my performances and stage presence.

Yeah, I took a couple of steps backwards, but for good reason. The pain was horrendous, and in my defence, I was informed that the pain would only last a year post-surgery. Obtaining a pain management team during COVID-19 was virtually impossible.

But I came off the medication again and recalibrated my attention to everything that I was devoted to, like music and this second book.

The withdrawal was simple as I had only been back on them for a month. Things were very uncertain. But I was at a place in my life where I was attempting to trust the process and timing of my life.

I mean, I hadn't gotten this far just to stop now ... right?

I like to believe this same mantra applied to everyone else during these difficult times!

Meanwhile, I was working on the post-production of my upcoming singles. I was on a mission to become more self-sufficient and independent. My aim was to obtain my own self-contained apartment close to the city with a city skyline where I no longer had to answer to anyone, nor walk on eggshells.

I simply yearned peace.

I did, however, socialise and go out with some new people just for some casual encounters and networking, but I wasn't wanting anything serious. In fact, I was simply seeking new friendships. Though I did go out with an Australian celebrity. This person wanted to see me again (for an intimate date), but I declined and suggested we remain friends – she didn't take this too well.

I wanted to rediscover myself and not get caught up in anything serious yet again. I was finally in a good frame of mind in terms of finding my own feet and independence once more. She was a decent egg. Most people would've jumped at the chance to be with her, but I was stepping into my own power and regardless of someone else's status and appeal, I knew I wanted to invest in myself.

I was also being mentored by a former Australian renowned artist and I was attaining valuable advice about progressing my career. He made much time for me, and we had many zoom calls whenever he travelled back and forth from country to country. I was highly grateful for the time he provided me, despite how busy he was.

A couple of old friends and I reconnected, and a lot of self-growth had taken place in the time we'd been apart. We were healthier in the realm of communication, and I was in a place where I was more independent and less reliant on others to fill a void within me. So, our friendship was more balanced and mutual.

Furthermore, a timely reconciliation occurred just when I was questioning the process once more. Out of the blue, Sharon reached out to me and apologised for what she put me through, especially during the timeframe of when my mother died. I found it to be a very honourable thing to do and I immediately forgave her. It was very healing and timely.

At this stage, I was in a better frame of mind in terms of growing pains and forgiveness. I could understand the human condition in more simpler terms, and I was less resentful toward people who had previously hurt me. I understood the phrase 'hurt people, hurt people'.

Of course, I was absolutely exhausted by all these teachings over the past two years (and this lifetime in general) but I was starting to set heathier boundaries for myself, and I started monitoring how people were treating me to prevent history from repeating itself and would immediately identify if something wasn't right.

I was too tired to put myself in toxic positions anymore. But things were different now. I was a stronger version of myself.

Still gentle and kind – but stronger!

Chapter 7

Give Me A Break!

I decided that 2022 would be a time for self-healing and accomplishing my goals. Despite many setbacks and self-doubt the only option was to rest here and there and attempt to proceed with my endeavours.

My faith was tested beyond comprehension and although I feel many could relate to the uncertainty that was ahead of them, in terms of pursuing their dreams during the pandemic, nobody knew how long it would last, and the economy was (of course) crashing as a result.

Just when I thought I was at the peak of finally rising above it all, I started to get depressed and had moments of losing my faith. It wasn't consistent as the journey to my next destination of enlightenment was not yet solidified. More work had to be done.

This was a turbulent time in finding my feet. I finally had the vision of what I wanted my life to be, including the WILL to make it happen. But good things take time. I just didn't know that then.

I had moments where I contemplated giving up on everything. I felt worthless; I had suicidal thoughts; I was immensely depressed and felt utterly alone on the journey I was facing. I saw no hope. I believed in my talents, but perhaps just not in the prospects of having any chance at using them. I was so tired and any luck in the current world we were living in appeared to be virtually non-existent.

Despite the network I had around me, I felt like no matter how hard anyone tried to make me feel better, their words just didn't align with what I believed and I needed to hear the most. But then again, everyone else was fighting their own battles. I had to remember that I need to be my own saviour in the end, as I had been many times before.

Of course, this was extremely difficult. Maintaining momentum and any form of ambition was extremely challenging for many.

I was so exhausted by everything that I'd endured. Regaining my energy proved to be difficult. I noticed I had slipped back in regard to the music that I was listening to and the food I was eating. I wasn't being kind to my mind and body. I was 52 kilos, and I wasn't even attempting to walk outside to smell the roses anymore.

I had become a hermit, and whenever I would eat it would only be via the means of a drive-thru restaurant. I had become lazy and unmotivated. I didn't want to be seen by anyone. I was embarrassed of myself and what I felt I'd become.

I was regressing again, but I knew I had no more time to waste. So, I started listening to affirmations again; I reached for my angel cards, burned incense, listened to positive music whenever I felt low and chose more nutritional food. It wasn't easy to commit to.

Some days I just wanted to remain stuck in my melancholy state and feel sorry for myself. Time was running out. I was 35 and the prospect of ever making a positive impression on the music industry was fleeting. I had to commit to doing the work once more, despite how deflated I felt.

If I'm honest, I didn't really like myself, especially after all the silly decisions I had previously made when I thought I knew better. I was disappointed about reverting to my old patterns and contradicting all that I believed I stood for.

Something that didn't help was that I was receiving more hate mail on social media. People would contact me, calling me a 'bludger' because I was on disability for my CPTSD and tell me that I had 'no talent'. That hurt.

I knew how hard I was working behind the scenes and if anyone had read my previous book then they'd know how hard I've worked outside of the workforce to contribute to humanity on a different scale.

I just had no income attached to this work to define my value in society in the eyes of others. Plus, I feared the workforce due to sexual assault and harassment I experienced when I was younger. We had no 'me too' movements back then.

(PS, you're still enough if you don't work!)

The last straw was when I had a minor car accident. I had twisted my arm in the steering wheel whilst making a U-turn, only to do a complete 180 and land on the island that divides the road.

My car was fine. But days after the car felt wonky to drive. I was driving to my rehearsals and other commitments when suddenly, one morning, three bolts from my front right tyre were missing. Eventually the wheel would come off its hinges. But not before I drove it home, very slowly. Thankfully, I was only one minute away from the parking lot of the apartment complex when I was escorted back home by two policemen in their car in order to make sure no accidents occurred and that I got my car in the car park safely.

My CPTSD flared beyond comprehension, and I needed to take two Valium to settle myself and prevent a panic attack . I'd already been through so much these past two years. I'd had enough, although in great appreciation, the policemen were lovely to me.

I had to swallow my pride and ask my housemate if he'd help me with my tyre. It was sufficiently awkward, especially considering I'd ended things with his relative.

The energy had been off for weeks. Nevertheless, he helped me replace my tyre with the spare from the boot.

I retraced my steps prior to the incident and I managed to find the three bolts that came off in the car park. Then I went to two auto shops where I was assisted by two beautiful humans free of charge. I cried and thanked them profusely.

I went and bought my housemate some chocolates, a card, and some kitchen decorative jars from the Reject Shop (something I knew he loved) in order to thank him. I honestly couldn't afford roadside assistance and I was genuinely grateful toward him. He wasn't responsive, though. I knew something was wrong. Nevertheless, I had $40 to my name, and I could feel a change was in the air.

An abrupt change.

I continued with the motions. My intuition proved to be right about my housemate.

I discovered that he had unfollowed me days prior on every social media network. I could sense it was coming as he was constantly complaining about something he wasn't happy with regarding our living situation.

And I'm talking very trivial things.

It was clearly in relation to his relative, no doubt about it. Understandably, he wasn't considering my side of the story despite my efforts to inform him of the severity in the nature of our differences and why it didn't work out. I corrected everything he wasn't happy with, though he found more trivial things to complain about. I could feel that he was just attempting to drive me out of the house.

Regardless, I displayed the utmost gratitude towards him and offered to be of any help to him in the future if need be, though he was non-responsive. It was triggering me because I'd already experienced the silent treatment in my previous social dynamic.

Days went by and I was tired of expressing concern for what my housemate thought of me. It was just too much. The cycle ended from this point onwards. I had to embrace my previous revelations from my first book.

I struggled and many days I entertained the idea of entirely giving up everything. I felt like one huge joke and was living with someone who constantly made me feel bad about everything I was doing in the house. I felt inadequate. No matter how many times I attempted to appease him, nothing worked. Granted, he was only 27 years old. He had a lot to learn about life.

But I had to make something out of all of this. There had to be meaning to all of this. I had to keep believing it wasn't for nothing. Otherwise, I'd just give up and all my hard work would have been for nothing!

And what a waste that would be.

Anyway, I had two headline shows coming up and I was anything but in the right frame of mind to exude confidence. I had to work on my mental health daily in order to get back into form for those upcoming events.

I decided to go out for the night to my old stomping ground which I'd played at years prior to the pandemic. I walked around and reminisced with joy in my heart. I even went to an old lesbian bar that I use to attend four years ago. It was very refreshing and nice being in solitude amongst it all. I was leisurely walking around the suburb just taking the night in.

I was offered free booze upon many bar entrances (countless times) but I was driving home and politely declined. But despite the fact that I drove there, I still didn't yearn to escape for once. If anything, I wanted to take it all in.

Look at that.

I wasn't feeling lonely for once.

I felt at peace with whatever was happening to me. It was a strange feeling because I've never been fully comfortable in my own company, and I've always felt alone wherever I was. But this time I felt if not okay, then at least enlightened by my progression.

When I returned home, I made a cup of chai tea and wrote down all the goals I wished to achieve in 2022. They were very modest and attainable.

One of them being that I wished to have my own apartment, similar to the one I was currently staying in. I absolutely adored it. I never wanted to share accommodation ever again. But the trick would be how to attain such a thing on a disability pension, although many people I knew had achieved it, so why couldn't I?

I'd never had my own safe haven and I loved an apartment life with a view. Why couldn't I attain that for myself? That was my main goal. I simply yearned peace! Oh, and a financial windfall to get myself out of debt and maintain financial security would be nice, preferably provided by either music or my books as I'd already worked extremely hard on everything for the past eight years and it would be nice to be recognised for that.

So, I attempted to manifest it. The following day, I decided to leave the apartment. I just felt so uncomfortable and unwanted there.

Despite the possibility of being homeless, I packed up all my belongings and placed them in my car on a boiling hot day with fear in my heart, tears in my eyes and no idea on where to go from there.

I called Jo and asked for a favour. Thankfully my guardian angel came through and allowed me to stay with her until I found a place of my own. It wasn't an easy exit. I shed many tears, attempted to navigate myself in an entirely new town again, updated all my details all over again and accepted that I'd taken a hundred steps backwards. But I knew it was coming. My housemate had just pushed me too far.

I had to sell a few more items for cash because I was so poor. It was scary. But I made a promise to myself that I would commit to saving and getting my own place in 2022.

That was my main priority, besides my headline shows and second book.

The one good thing out of all of this was that my resilience was in check and on point – for the most part. I did have some ebbing and flowing of emotion, which was natural provided the circumstances.

I have to say, the transition of environment was eye opening. I was now living in a suburban home filled with love and warmth as opposed to a stale city apartment with toxic energy circulating the place. Not to suggest every apartment contains that vibe.

But this transition cemented my initial feelings revolving the environment I wanted to make for myself going forward. I was no longer walking on eggshells. I could be me. I went from a city apartment with a view to a loving suburban home filled with hope.

It made me reflect on what truly matters in the end – not the destination, but merely the feelings your environment exudes. Although I still wanted a studio apartment for myself in the future, my intention would be to fill it with the same energy Jo's house exuded.

Days later, my gut feelings regarding my former housemate would truly manifest. He sent me one of the most abusive emails I'd ever received in my life, and trust me, I've received a few unpleasant messages in my time. Everything he said about me was furthest from the truth … all but one thing.

No, I didn't have an organic following. We mere 'nobodies' needing to 'appear as if we have traction and interest in order to get somewhere'. Well, so I thought so at the time. Regardless, that was the only truth in his email. But that was nothing.

He stated, and I quote, 'Let me educate you Saffire.' Then proceeded to say I should rename my book 'Maybe you should look in the mirror – a story about the degenerate'.

Lovely, right?

It was the vile names he called me and how he completely

attacked my entire character and everything I stood for that really hurt.

The lowest thing was being told that my father was right to leave me as a child because I was 'worthless scum' and he wasn't missing out on much. Then he proceeded to say that I walk around life as if the world owes me something and that my life is pitiful and embarrassing.

Then he accused me of saying filthy comments to him whilst living in his space, which is far from anything I stand for. He even went so low as to send me a one-cent bank transfer with a description calling me a 'filthy pillow thief' because I took two pillows and a bed sheet that my friend had bought for me. I mean, really? Who does that?

I could say a lot about him here in terms of how hypocritical everything he said to me was, but I won't stoop to his level. All I'll say is that everything but the paid followers comment was untrue and a mere reflection of something he was feeling about himself in the end. Which I empathise with but won't stand for.

I didn't deserve that treatment.

I contemplated suicide every day, but I kept saying, 'I haven't come this far, just to come this far'.

In all honestly, my former housemate and his recent exchange of his opinions toward me only confirmed my intuition and proceedings in relation to acting on leaving that apartment in the first place.

The only regret I have here is that I tried so hard for him to like me. I overcompensated when it was never truly me, it was him! It really gutted me that I was in this situation, yet again. Everything ahead was so uncertain, and I was *scared*.

I kept looking back and trying to piece everything together on where I'd gone so terribly wrong in my life. But I knew this wouldn't help me move forward. The only option I had was to drown or swim, so I swam frickin hard!

Out of all these trials and tribulations the past two years, the roller-coaster had to end with me! I committed to my band rehearsals, did a backing track vocal recording session with my producer for my upcoming shows and sought a permanent place of residency for myself, whilst keeping my head high. Despite how exhausted and depleted I felt. The show had to go on, and trust me, the pressure was brewing.

It was time to revive my life!

Chapter 8

And Just Like That ...

I had to find my own safe haven as soon as possible and prepare for two headline shows with venue operators increasing the pressure for numbers.

That very week, for the first time in my life, I was applying to rental properties for myself and myself only! It was a struggle and a hustle, especially during a global pandemic. I was discriminated against for not having a rental history and for being on disability support, despite the fact that my bank records disclosed how capable I was of paying rent on a regular basis.

I was truly being tested in every way possible: by hate, rejection, uncertainty, pressure, poverty, isolation (minus my beautiful angel Jo). Everything was crumbling and I was holding the fort to set a clear motion in place for a future I wasn't even sure existed for me anymore.

Yes, I was sleeping on a couch. But I had a beautiful friend who truly was there for me when nobody else was ... and for that, I could only be the most grateful. Jo inspired me every day with her stories of prevailing against adversity and reminded me so much of my mum in many respects. It was truly a blessing being placed beside her in hospital a year prior to writing this very chapter.

My one goal in 2022 was to cement my own accommodation so I could focus primarily on music and my writing. Jo offered for me to stay rent free for several months, but I wasn't going to take advantage of that, nor her for that matter. I really wanted to prove to myself that I could do it on my own.

So I sold my car, applied for copious properties and I budgeted like mad! It was a shitstorm. But I was determined to get my own apartment even if it meant selling my car. It had to be done. I craved independence for the first time in my life.

I sold a lot of my possessions online, in order to gather savings for a bond. I lost everything once more – but I was okay with it this time. So long as there was a positive purpose toward it. I never had to hold onto faith in the universe more than this time.

But still, this was nothing in comparison to what I'd already endured. I guess my body and soul were just tired. My stamina was fleeting in existence, although I did notice that my rehearsals were sounding fiercer, and I was singing certain lines with more conviction because I was truly living the words I'd written.

Later that week, I played my two headline shows despite all my nerves and uncertainty. Though I had immense self-doubt during both performances, I continued to push through.

Just for something different, I decided to participate in the Melbourne midsummer pride festival to change up my general routine and try something different. I joined the Latin American & Hispanic Rainbow Community march as I have some biological heritage in Spain. It was so fulfilling to be a part of something so uniting. I stepped out of my comfort zone in this regard. The previous Sydney Mardi Gras I attended was with a former partner many years ago. This time I walked with people … but alone. It was empowering.

I had many date proposals and people wanting to connect with me at this time, but I was determined to do it alone. I was more mindful of the energy around me and the patterns I'd previously practiced and repeated that kept continuing the cause and effect in my life.

It had to stop, starting with my choices and attitude.

I chose to be alone rather than surround myself with distractions, external validation, and false security. For the first time in my life, I didn't want anyone to save me or tell me everything I longed to hear. I had already been disappointed enough. I learned throughout all those experiences that at the end of the day the only person who was keeping me alive and well-grounded was ultimately myself! I saw the teachings and valued them, as hard as they were at times.

Almost everyone saw me as the damsel in distress, incapable of surviving life without them.

But I could and I would!

I was reviving my life *alone!*

I found I was more assertive, less afraid of stepping on toes and more conscious of what I wanted going forward. I had a vision, and nothing was going to break it – not even my own fears.

And just like that, I scored an apartment of my very own! I did it.

Yes, it was only a lease, and it came with a few heated discussions between the former tenant and myself, but finally I was going out on my own and seizing the opportunity to conquer this world without anyone holding my hand.

I would demonstrate good rental history to prevent sharing with others before I attain my own apartment one day.

Literally five years from my mother's death, I moved my entire remaining life into my very own apartment all on my own. I also set everything up independently. I sought absolutely no assistance. I was so proud of myself. I had a beautiful view of St Kilda on the top floor of a beautiful apartment complex. It was everything I ever wanted for myself. Although it wasn't permanent, I was one step closer to my vision of my future.

As a thank you for having me, I took Jo to see a J.Lo film and, after Jo's biopsy, I made sure her dinner was taken care of because I was so grateful for this woman. Without her, I would have been on the street.

I had never felt more empowered than I did from this point.

I promised myself that I'd *never* move in with a future partner before owning my own place. I'd finally learned my lessons and I would never allow myself to be left destitute and homeless again.

I'm loving my independence and I'm so proud of how far I've come. I now know that I *can* do it on my own!

I'm also enjoying cooking for myself – something I never thought I'd be able to achieve. Reason being, I almost burned down my mother's housing commission house when I was young due to a glitch in the gas oven. Since then, I refrained from ever going near an appliance of gas oven or stove top. But I faced my fear one cold winter's night and cooked myself a healthy stir-fry.

Ah, the little wins in life.

Again, I still don't know what the future holds but at least I can say I've given it my all and if I died tomorrow, I'd be proud that I left two honest books behind and some music to help people feel less alone in the realm of adversity.

Chapter 9

Reviving My Life

Upon finishing this book, we lost our beautiful Blaise (the publisher of Busybird). She was the reason I'm able to share my stories to this very day. The writing community, her friends and family were understandably devastated. I still cannot fathom that I saw her just weeks prior to finishing this book. She was so lively and full of laughter. Grief and a funeral were not something we anticipated after what had already been a tough two years – especially regarding Blaise. It's still inconceivable.

I remember applying her false eyelashes before an event and us laughing at how uncoordinated I was in the process. I hold many warm and loving feelings for her, and I know she'd be proud of us all.

I also contracted a very strong case of COVID-19. It was horrendous. I wondered to myself, was this it? After everything I'd survived, was COVID going to be the thing that takes me out?

I was hospitalised because of the constant coughing and breathing difficulties which aggravated my ribs. It was nothing like your common flu. It took me two weeks to recover, and I still have some side effects.

I was in so much pain that I resorted to the prescribed combined CBD Oil.

On one occasion I took 0.05 mil extra and had my very first experience of being 'high' based on the combination of THC and CBD that was infused in the bottle.

I remember calling my friend on my mobile and seeking her advice, and whether I should call an ambulance.

My heartrate was increasing by the minute, my speech was becoming slurred and I felt like my bones were about to jump out from underneath my skin. It was ONE of the most unsettling and horrific experiences I'd ever endured.

In my chemically enhanced state, my friend's voice was very slow and I remember being frustrated at how long she was taking to reply in between my questions. I felt like I was speaking like a robot.

Haha! In hindsight, the experience now makes me laugh.

Little did I know I'd be falling asleep not long after that phone call.

Needless to say, I developed an aversion to the oil, threw it out and never ordered another batch again.

Since coming off all my medications, and now being a year since my two rib surgeries, I've gained back all of my weight. I'm currently 62 kilos, which is a lot healthier than 47 kilos. It was hard to adjust initially, but I'm learning to love my body in all its glory.

To be honest, I'm just grateful to be alive. I almost died. I've stared death in the face and I'd rather be healthy than near death's door.

I made two new friends that eventuated into dates earlier that year. I was lonely living on my own and I was conscious that I needed to get out and be more social in order to avoid becoming a hermit.

I didn't take the dates too seriously, though. I wasn't looking for love. But these stories need to be shared as they're a good indication I was finally standing in my convictions.

One date led to me having my keys stolen in order to hold me hostage because I wouldn't have sex with her.

It was a surreal experience. She was drunk and grew needy and almost violent, until she unfortunately suffered a psychotic breakdown.

I talked to her calmly and rationally, more concerned about her well-being than the fact that I couldn't get my keys back, and that I had no spare keys.

I was concerned for my welfare, but was able to connect with her long enough to help her, as well as retrieve my keys. The episode was a mirror to me – that we can chase the things we want until we lose all sense of reason.

And the second date led me to being punched in the stomach. That punch completely triggered my CPTSD and winded the crap out of me, not to mention it flared the pain in my ribs.

It was an innocent demonstration of how strong this particular woman was in regard to her kung fu expertise. Granted, I suggested displaying her maneuvers but I suggested in the air, and not into my stomach.

She insisted nonetheless.

When she saw I was triggered, she proceeded to speak about the method of approach she just used, whilst disregarding the tears rolling down my eyes.

She further told me that in the mastery of kung fu, students and teachers are trained to disassociate from their emotions.

I told her, 'I'm not a student.'

But she couldn't see my point of view.

There's no doubt her strength, purpose, and conviction are tools that help her in her job as a Life Coach, and also make her very good at what she does, but it's also evidence that we can all sometimes be blind to things we don't want to see – in this case, that she'd hurt me.

It took her four days to apologise, and it took a 'sex dream' of the two of us to make her realise she'd messed up.

She said (and I quote), 'I saw this beautiful fragile side to you and it made me realise what a fool I'd been.'

No judgement here ... But really?

My word.

The good thing to all of this: I was adamant to not repeat my old patterns. I was merely exploring my options and discovering new limitations and implementing my newly established boundaries.

Here I was, 36 years old and I was finally practising what I preached. I wasn't settling anymore. I promised myself that I would be best friends with the person who is destined to be my 'end game'. There'd be no more rushing into things without truly getting to know someone.

Lastly, another valued connection I made was my publisher who took over the reigns regarding our beloved Blaise van Hecke, who was our former publisher and who we lost earlier in 2022.

He guided me through the final stages of this second book and welcomed every facet of me that unravelled towards the end of completing this book. Many tears were shed. We both supported each other through some hard times – him, losing his best friend, and me catching up with my trauma.

He stood by me when everything was starting to hit me tenfold.

We've become very good friends since and I like to believe something good came out of our loss.

He's not just my publisher, I regard him as a good friend now – a confidante that is never afraid to provide me the truth when seeking.

I'm so grateful for all of these connections. They arrived just when the past thirty-six years had hit me and it was time to receive some emotional support during this time period. I'd done a lot of unpacking and it was bound to creep up on me. I'm grateful for everyone's patience and kindness.

Although some days were hard on my own, I was determined to stop my previous patterns and not band-aid, nor fill my cup with quick appeasing distractions. I was sitting in the uncomfortable.

On my birthday, Sam, an old childhood friend, got in contact with me. It was like no time had passed. We believe both our deceased parents orchestrated our connection again via the means of TikTok.

I came up on her #fyp and, trust me, I still don't have a lot of followers, so the odds were unusual.

We never realised up until many discussions that we were both struggling with similar battles behind closed doors in our younger years, though we were just too nervous to speak to each other about it. In hindsight, this makes sense due to the lack of support there was back then for people of our demographic.

I'm also in contact with an old school friend who was my first female crush. We both ended up gay. What are the odds? But she's in a happy relationship and we talk every week.

I never thought I'd ever have people in my life that knew me from the very beginning and are still a consistent in my life today. Trust me. They've seen all facets of me, yet still stuck around.

I had two second cousins come out of the woodwork, stayed with one of them numerous times this year, and I'm very close with the other. I'm starting to attract my tribe and, for that, I'm grateful.

I've grown so much this year. I believe I'm attracting the right people in my life today because I've come into my own. My consistent dedication toward my evolution of self, has led me to the right people for me at this stage in my life.

I'm hopeful it'll proceed as such – provided I maintain my newfound perspective on life and never lose sight of my authenticity and what truly matters.

Sharon came back into my life. It was a lot for me after all she put me through. But I knew she needed me at this stage in her life for serious factors. I couldn't turn her away. It's not in my nature.

She was in a complex situation and needed my help. I gave her money to stay in a safe place for a couple of nights and made sure she had food.

I also attended her mother's funeral. It was the first time I'd ever seen a dead body (in the flesh), as it was an open coffin. Two funerals in two months was enough for me to implement the reality of just how short life can be. The day of her mother's funeral was hard – not only for her, but dare I say, for me.

I hadn't seen Sharon since she abandoned me after my mother's death five years ago – she was smiling while I was crying and grieving. She verbally abused me and abandoned me when I needed her the most, yet here I was being there for her. It was a lot. I thought I was completely over it and healed, but there was some residue left.

I also couldn't help but feel sorry for my own mother, knowing that she never had that level of quality and a turn out for her send off, like Sharon's mum did. Her funeral was fit for royalty.

I know it wasn't the time to make comparisons, but I'm human, and the thought did pop up. It upset me that my mother was never appreciated and loved like that.

Of course, I composed myself, pushed my feelings aside and remained supportive. But when I returned home, a well of emotions poured out of me and I unravelled. I was so upset that the only legacy my mother has left was through me.

I decided that I never wanted to make the same mistakes my mother made. She never felt like she was enough and that narrative kept reflecting in her life up until the day she died.

The only way I could carry her memory on with the respect that it deserves was through my own discernment and how much I decided to respect and value myself going forward.

I also wanted to help people and give back to a community that helped me when I was down and out. Like particular food charities that delivered me boxes of groceries and essentials when I had COVID.

When the floods in NSW occurred and the war in Ukraine started, I also donated to the Australian Red Cross, the

Salvation Army and other charities supporting these crises. At that point, I didn't care anymore. I just wanted peace and to be generous after everything we had all endured during the pandemic. What else could anyone do to help? I think these disasters humbled many people – well, most of us.

Upon reconnecting with my childhood friends and people from my past, I decided to come home to Sydney for a week to catch up with everyone.

It was very healing for all of us.

I saw my former mentor (in the city). He now has dementia.

I knew I'd never forgive myself if I didn't see him before it got worse. So he was first on my list to visit.

Witnessing his decline in person was confronting and heartbreaking. He had once been articulate and generated such energy. Now he was frail, vague and had difficulty keeping up with conversation.

In our phone calls and texts throughout the last year, he had mistaken me for his lover, although we'd never had such a relationship.

This was triggering for me for many reasons but I had to remember the man I once knew was no longer. He was unable to control his thoughts and his memory wasn't as sharp or trustworthy as it once was.

I knew I had to compartmentalise my emotions and not take what was happening too heart. It was an irreversible condition that was primarily impacting him and the people who cared for him.

Still, he was in good spirits and thankfully remembered our musical endeavours in the early stages of my music career. I was grateful he remembered me at all.

I empathise with those who're experiencing far worse adverse reactions to this awful condition.

I then came home to the Central Coast and was greeted by Sam, my best friend from childhood.

It was like no time had passed. I was introduced to the beautiful family she had created (they now call me Aunty Saff) and we spent many days together.

I then met up with my high school crush and we had the best day running amok around the entrance (the Central Coast) playing pokies, going to the arcade and drinking our favourite spirits over some hilarious bantering.

I spent two nights in solitude at a motel that Mum and I always wanted to go to but could never afford. I enjoyed the spa bath and looked up at the sunny sky that was, and smiled knowing that Mum would be happy to see me enjoying myself and that I've reunited with all of the originals from the beginning.

I walked along the beach where Mum's ashes were scattered and spoke to her on numerous occasions. I felt her presence and that it was filled with pride with how far I'd come on my journey thus far.

When I returned to the city on my final day, prior to boarding my train trip back to Melbourne, I caught up with one important person from my musical journey – a long-standing friend I'd made when I first commenced my live performances in Sydney eight years ago.

The contrast in being in each individual's presence really highlighted how time is linear and that age, is indeed, just a number.

We all still carried hope in our hearts, a childlike enthusiasm yet wisdom to combat the unknown.

It was a treasured adventure to finalise the year that was and upon completing this book.

It made me realise that we're all in this together and we're all experiencing life from a different starting point, yet striving to reach the same destination: inner contentment, and inner peace.

Honestly, even though the trip was very rewarding on a spiritual level, it was also taxing on an emotional and mental level. I cried almost every night releasing elements of myself that always thought I wasn't enough.

Now I knew this was not the case (ever) and realising all the years I'd wasted doubting my worth was the creator of my turbulent reality.

I came back to Melbourne a changed person. Forever more. That trip healed a part of my inner child.

All I can say is ... yes, life is hard. But I believe that there's still hope for many of us. I don't believe we're being punished. I believe there's meaning in everything we're experiencing no matter how wrong it may appear to be. It's not a punishment.

Someday, I believe it will all make sense, and we'll finally gain world peace.

Call me a fool, but I believe.

Something to remember is that whenever someone puts you down or makes you feel worthless based on discrimination (of any kind), and you react and attempt to prove them wrong, you're ultimately continuing the problem without even realising.

You're already enough in this moment of your evolution – there's nothing to prove! We need to get off this treadmill of life and the constant grind, and let ourselves off the hook in order to be *something* or *someone*. Why can't we just *be*? Every generation has the same issue regarding societal standards and with each projection it creates a ripple effect destroying the generation to come.

Let me tell you something: most people who attain status and power aren't happy. Trust me, I've mixed with the best of them. They're absolutely miserable because they didn't chase those ambitions for the right reasons. It was to prove someone wrong. Then that continues for generations to come, causing immense segregation and heartbreak.

What would you be spending all your money on if those people you call 'the little people' who make your food and coffee didn't exist? Without them you wouldn't have any luxuries. There's always someone making our life a little easier, whether we realise it or not. Especially your garbage man! Without him, you're stuck with a pile of garbage in your house. Everyone matters. It's time we all treated everyone as equal so that worldly issues stop reoccurring.

It can stop with us, right now, by choosing to respect everyone's position in life. We're all coming from a different perspective and one person's circumstances aren't always applicable to another person's circumstances. It's time to be mindful of this and stop projecting belief systems onto others to accommodate to your own belief system. It's not applicable for everyone.

Forgive those who aren't learning at the same speed to you. Some people have massive distractions taking place that's aggravating their evolution of self. It's not personal! People are at war with themselves – not you! Consider this, and that's when the real magic will take place.

Remember, you're *more* than enough, and you're doing great! Being human is hard work!

I'm thankful that I just survived. If I thrive, I'm grateful for that too. But it's important to acknowledge that simply functioning in such a dysfunctional world is a massive win!

So, pat yourself on the back for getting this far! It's one crazy ride.

I believe we're all teachers. Guiding each other back home. To our core essence.

Just recently, I had a profound and productive conversation with a pastor that worked within a community that I'm now connecting with, on a weekly basis.

I remember his arms were folded carrying a stoic demeanour.

He told me that he likes to challenge people.

I asked him why is that?

He replied, 'Because people need to be challenged'

I sat back in my chair and calmly said, 'The thing that I've learned in life is that not everyone is comfortable with sitting in uncomfortable truths. So therefore challenging it with tough love doesn't always necessarily align with those who're not ready for change.'

He told me he had studied psychology.

I further proceeded to tell him (with love) from my own personal life experience and education regarding the human condition, that his body language and demeanour was coming across very intimidating, and that not many people would feel safe under his guidance and lecture.

I said, 'You'd attract more people if you softened your approach.'

Here I was instructing a pastor/teacher on how to communicate to general folk. Haha. The irony. But also very valid in regards to my point about humanity and how we can correct it with just a change of perspective and to stop relying on status and power, in order to define our worth in the world.

Feedback is a blessing. We all teach each other something.

He willingly took on my suggestions within an instant and I saw the power dynamics between a young woman (with very little education) and an older man (with plenty) change his mindset and body language. He became more engaged, approachable and curious to ascertain how I knew this.

I told him, 'I've been you. I've been the teacher and I've been the student. We all have. But a position of authority separates us.'

This is what labels and stigmas do. They segregate us and prevents us from truly connecting.

So, how can we make peace with the world?

It starts by striving for peace within our own world – that's where the real work needs to be done.

I know, its easier said than done. But I promise, with practice, there's a chance for resolve.

The issue is that there's no simplified information on how to truly love yourself. We're just told to do 'mirror work' and 'affirmations', which are positive things, but they're not necessarily effective for everyone and very time consuming.

I believe it's through releasing the ego essence of self that the process to reaching the destination of self love can be achieved.

Therefore you're able to love others that, in fact, prior, you would've probably felt apprehensive to ever trust or even care for.

It's important to not associate the word 'ego' as a negative connotation. It's merely a tool that's used to protect oneself from harm, judgement or disappointment – among many other triggers.

The irony is, we protect ourselves from the very thing that causes pain.

Refraining from judging other people and situations which you don't understand will diminish any judgement or shame you place upon yourself.

When you learn to accept all the parts of yourself that the ego is inclined to reject, you begin to embrace and accept your true self and the world around you, bringing everything into perfect harmony.

My advice to all the young lovers of the world: try falling in love with yourself before loving another person.

It's true what they say – how can you love someone if you cannot even love yourself?

I myself can say I have never been in love despite how deeply I felt for everyone upon my journey. Marilyn was the closest I ever got. But we didn't love ourselves. So it was virtually impossible.

I honour and treasure this gift of rediscovery myself. I've learned a lot about myself upon finishing this book and I'm grateful to have been on such an extraordinary journey thus far.

I now know when I do fall in love, it'll be with a best friend.

My person.

Wherever they are, I know time has prevented us from being together because we have to grow while we're apart. I know I wouldn't have been ready.

I'm glad for this intermission.

Just something in addition to add for those who suffer from mental health obstacles (like myself) and tend to receive rejection regarding this matter: please understand, it's not personal.

What I have learned is that some people might not have the capacity to withstand the storm that coexists in your reality that you experience within yourself on a daily basis.

If you get triggered by a partner, a friend or a work colleague, I have found that some people's reaction to your reaction is merely based on either a negative past association (unrelated to the present situation) or due to the fact that they tend to carry your reaction/trigger stemming from your trauma, as a personal reflection of themselves.

Your trigger response can sometimes leave a person feeling like they're the (original) predator/abuser – the person who originally inflicted the wound upon you in the first place.

This can be uncomfortable for the person on the receiving end. So they're inclined to retreat.

It's self preservation. It's not personal.

Everyone has limitations and that is okay. With the right people aligned with your journey and IF you're ready, nothing will interfere with an authentic connection going forward.

Everyone is enough ...

Just some people are not serving your journey and vice versa.

Every interaction serves its purposes in the end, even if it is a fleeting moment in time.

If you're open to the concept, hindsight eventually demonstrates why that experience was crucial toward your healing journey and overall growth.

I'm no longer scared to be alone.

I enjoy it.

I'm loving myself a little more everyday and now when I possibly meet my person it won't be a *need*.

It'll be a *want*.

Solidarity is a gift. It's the roadmap to returning home to yourself.

Food for thought.

I hope my two books have resonated with you in a positive way, and if you can take anything away from my candid reflections please take this … stop doubting your worth!

This is Saffire-Rose Fletcher, over and out! Xx

Acknowledgements

I'd like to thank everyone in this book who contributed to my development these past two years in order for this book to be possible.

I'd also like to thank Jo Foster for taking me in when I had nowhere else to go and for loving me unconditionally, when i was struggling to love myself.

I'd like to thank Blaise van Hecke, who believed in my first book, interviewed me in her spare time and tolerated how turbulent my process was. You're forever missed.

Thank you Brooklyn O'Connell. She did a fantastic job in establishing the perspective in which I was coming from, and was always so patient with my specifications. I know she'll do great things as an editor.

And last but not least, a massive thankyou to Les Zig, for taking this book and helping me polish it with tender loving care, whilst contending with his own grief.

Les Zig is a phenomenal human who provided a safe space for me to be vulnerable and listened to many of my infamous tangents.

I'm grateful for this journey. It is life changing. I wouldn't change a thing.

Resources

If you've been triggered by any of the things discussed in this book, here are some helpful resources.

Lifeline: 13 11 14 or lifeline.org.au
Beyond Blue: 1300 22 46 36 or beyondblue.org.au
Kids Helpline: 1800 55 18 00 or kidshelpline.com.au
Headspace: 1800 650 890 or headspace.org.au

This is not a self-help book.

This is a story about healing, self-acceptance and overcoming adversity. It's not always pretty and that's how it's supposed to be, so that we can grow and understand who we are, and what we truly need in our lives.

It's also a story about learning to understand damaged people, finding forgiveness and rising above the prejudices of others.

Follow Saffire's journey as she navigates love, loss, relationships, coming out, music and growing up in a troubled neighbourhood, alongside being diagnosed with Complex PTSD in the midst of a pandemic.

Notes

Notes

Notes

Notes

Notes

Notes

Notes

Notes

Notes

Notes

Notes

Notes

Don't forget you can find me here ...

Facebook:
www.facebook.com/saffireroseofficial/

Instagram:
www.instagram.com/saffirerosefletcher_official

YouTube:
www.YouTube.com/saffirerosefletcher

www.ingramcontent.com/pod-product-compliance
Lightning Source LLC
Chambersburg PA
CBHW071125130526
44590CB00056B/2281